POCKET GUIDE TO VACATION RENTAL PROFITABILITY

12 Simple Steps to Success

Hal Rogers

This book is dedicated to two people:

The first is Ellen Keene; we hired her as our cleaning lady, and she immediately promoted herself to Guest Relations Manager.

The second is you; may its contents serve you as well as they have us...

Table of Contents

INTRODUCTION

So, you own a vacation rental property, have a property you are thinking about converting to a vacation rental, or you are thinking about buying a property and making it a vacation rental. A vacation rental property can be profitable and enjoyable to own; it can also be a costly liability. To a significant degree, the decisions you make before you post your listing and the actions you take afterwards will determine which it will be for you.

Anyone who starts a business begins with grand visions of profitability. It's possible to turn those visions into reality, but making a business profitable takes money, time, effort, commitment and, most of all, the right mindset as to customers, clients or, in this case, guests. Unless you bring guests to your property and then favorably impress them, failure is likely going to be your experience. Your rental can sit empty while the one next to you or down the street is consistently rented. Taking the proper approach to management and operation can have you saying to inquirers, *"I'm so sorry; those dates are already booked. Perhaps you'd like to lock in dates now for next year!"* How you approach the marketplace will be a function of the way you think, and can be the difference between success and failure.

Short term rentals and vacation rentals are different things and the approach to managing them is different. If yours is a short-term rental, some of what is included here will be helpful to you, but this guide is geared towards vacation rentals. In it, you will learn what gets guests to your property initially and, just as important, how to leave them not just considering, but decided, to come back and visit again!

In this guide, you will learn what a profit-making mindset is, but as you will see, it is counterintuitive. Your reason for owning a vacation rental is financial, but a focus on money is not the answer. That would be the worst thing you could do. In this guide you will learn a better focus, one that will create profits, but as a byproduct. When you adopt that focus, you'll experience the joy of watching it all work the way you want it to! Commit to learn what that focus is, adopt it, and maintain it, no matter what, and you will short track your path to success.

To get good at anything, one must learn what works and practice it. In sports, business, science, and any other field of endeavor, best practices get best results. In my career, I spent twenty-plus years focusing on money, and I got what that gets. Frustrated, disillusioned, and practically broke, I finally discovered what gets not only desired financial results, but also personal satisfaction and beautiful relationships, things that make life enjoyable and satisfying.

The below photo reflects what you want your focus to be. Keep reading; you'll see why...

OWN NEAR A HIGH-DEMAND DESTINATION

It is much more likely that you will attract guests to your vacation rental property if it is located in an area where there is something they want to see or do. Initial demand won't be for your property; it will be for the attraction(s) in your area. Lots of people coming to Disney World means lots of people needing a place to sleep, but they don't rent in Orlando because they want to spend the night in Orlando. Tourists plan, first, to go to Disney World; then they turn their attention to finding a suitable place for them and their family and/or friends to lay their heads at night.

When there is a group of people involved, it can cost less, per person, to book a vacation rental than to put everyone in the group in hotel rooms. A couple or a small group may be willing to pay a little more for a whole house where their surroundings aren't limited to a couple of beds and a shower. Your job is to attract those people already planning a trip to your area, and then to give them reasons to want to come back, specifically, to your place!

Location can't be overemphasized. On any given night, there will be more people looking for a rental in Orlando, Florida than there will be in Claxton, Georgia. There is nothing wrong with Claxton, but Mickey Mouse doesn't live there!

The cost to buy a property in the vicinity of an attraction will be more, but it will rent for more, and if managed properly, should more than cover that higher cost. Properties directly on the Rainbow River in Dunnellon, Florida cost more than properties across the street from those properties, but they command higher rents.

Everyone doesn't have an attraction as big as Disney World in their area. If this is the case, get as close as you can to whatever there is in your area that people are likely to visit. While it is better if it's a major vacation attraction, if there isn't one, there are still other options. It could be the beach, the mountains, a body of water known for good fishing, a historical site, a university, even a hospital known for specialty treatment. Anything people are likely to visit counts. If there is such in your area, purchase a property as close to it as you can.

If you already have a property you are thinking of converting, and you aren't in an area with an attraction, you might want to do some research to find if there is sufficient demand to support a short-term rental property. If a few short-term rents won't exceed monthly rent for a long-term tenant, conversion isn't a good idea.

Should you decide to have a non-vacation property, some of what follows will apply, but only minimally. If you are buying in a low-demand area, or are converting an existing property in a low-demand area, you aren't as likely to have repeat guests, and that property isn't going to rent at the same rates

as will a high demand vacation area property. What you will need to decide is which your non-vacation property is best suited for, short-term or long-term rental.

LIST ON THE MOST POPULAR ONLINE LISTING SITES

There are many ways to advertise any product, but the proven media for vacation rental advertising is online listing sites. This is where people go when they are looking for a vacation rental property. There are several options from which to choose, and new ones spring up occasionally. Choose wisely - your ability to get your property in front of first-time guests will, in large part, depend on your decisions.

Some sites offer free subscriptions, but they do so only because they don't have a substantial position in the marketplace. They don't have as many listings as the big players do and they aren't spending nearly as much on advertising. This means they aren't driving as many potential renters to the properties on their sites as are the major players. Also, once a site reaches a certain number of listings, they are likely going to add a subscription fee, and, at some point, raise that fee. After all, this correlates with their purpose in offering services.

Cost isn't the only issue when listing online. It is no small task to list, with property descriptions, photos, and other listing details. Your site must synchronize with other sites you are using to prevent double bookings. Your calendar on one site must fill in the dates when someone books on another one you are using and there can be issues with syncing. Free is no bargain if it isn't bringing you guests or is burdensome to manage the listing.

My experience suggests that it' is best to use only the two most popular sites, Airbnb and Vrbo. They are the gorillas in the industry. They have the name recognition and the advertising budget, and these are the two primary factors necessary to get in front of and attract lots of potential guests. For our properties on the Rainbow River in Dunnellon, FL, based on results,  they have delivered the most cost-effective advertising available.

 Listing on Airbnb and Vrbo costs more, and you pay or don't play, but they perform. Airbnb has the name recognition; virtually every person I have ever told personally about our two rentals, has asked, *"Do you list them on Airbnb?"* Yahoo Finance says that Expedia Group, which includes Vrbo, is the powerhouse in the vacation rental advertising arena. If you watch television or spend any time on your computer, you have likely seen their ads.

I have listed previously on other sites, but they proved to be more trouble than they were worth. My original thinking was anyplace I get one more booking is one more than I would have had. However, they are burdensome and create more opportunity for syncing issues.

Additionally, it is likely that I would have booked those dates on Airbnb or Vrbo anyway. So, I dropped those sites and stayed exclusively with Airbnb and Vrbo.

LEAD WITH PRICE...
FOLLOW WITH EXTRAORDINARY!

Guests are attracted to a property with exceptional Reviews. The day you list your property, and before it has been in service for a while, you either won't have any Reviews or will have few. Thus, you must have another way to get guests to your property, even if it costs you. Before you can do the other things included in this guide, you must have people show up. The way to do this is with below market rates.

While everyone appreciates a bargain, intelligent shoppers aren't looking for "cheap". If what they are being offered is value, at a lower than market price, they know there must be a reason for it. Also, that reason must be one they consider reasonable. Otherwise, they will be skeptical, wonder what they are overlooking, and they likely won't book.

Therefore, you need to fill in the gaps for them. You do that with this heading: **"New Listing - Introductory Rate"**. Potential guests aren't interested in spending their vacation in some dump, at any price, but this is something at which a reasonable number of people will be willing to take a look. If your property photos do their job, you'll get inquiries; if you handle the inquiries correctly, you'll get bookings.

In any industry, it isn't possible to sustain an offering of the highest quality product at the lowest available price, thus, your initial strategy is a short-term one. You'll only offer below market rates until people you attract provide you the Reviews you need to attract guests at market rates. You can't compete at market rates from day one, because travelers are reluctant to rent properties without Reviews! Unless you are in an area with more demand than there is supply, you must be willing to do what gets an initial number of guests to come without Reviews and the only thing that will do this is low rates.

Below market rates properly promoted on listing sites will get a number of first-time visitors quicker than anything else an owner can do.

Once your property has twenty-five or thirty 5-Star Reviews with "rave" comments, it won't matter that those guests came because of price, and you can ease rates up to competitive levels without price resistance. However, once you have the Reviews, and your rates are comparable with similar listings in your area, you don't have to settle for just getting a fair share of the bookings. You can get a high percentage of the potential bookings. **The way to get a disproportionally higher percentage of available bookings is to make certain that the Reviews potential guests are seeing on your property are disproportionally better than any of the other Reviews they are seeing.**

Guests have a reason for picking the property they pick. The information they have on which to base their decision is property location, your description and photos, and Reviews. All of these are obviously important but Reviews provide the most opportunity for significant emotional impact, and that impact can be positive or negative. Also, third party reviews are seen as more objective than what you say about your rental property.

This is your chance to shine, so you don't want to be satisfied just getting good Reviews, or even with just 5-Star Reviews. What you want potential guests to see are extraordinary 5-Star Reviews! You want them to see raves, maybe not even about the property, but about the hosts, the personal communication, the exceptional things the host(s) did, in other words, about their experience at your vacation rental!

Therefore, once guests come, you must give them an incredible experience, one which will translate into an incredible 5-Star Review. Beginning with your first rental, you want to deliver a list of extraordinary guest experiences. This is the only way a cadre of guests will not just exhibit satisfaction, but will report an exceptional experience following their stay. When this occurs, future guests will take notice and follow. Attract with value; deliver an unprecedented encounter. Once you have done this, you can bring your rates up sufficiently to support your operation and to make a profit. The surprising thing is how easy it is to do this, and you're about to learn how it is done...

CHOOSE A MANAGERIAL APPROACH

A major decision for vacation rental owners is what approach to take as to property management. You must consider whether you are willing to do what is necessary to obtain over-the-top results, and whether or not you have the time to do so.

Additionally, you or someone you hire will have to clean the property between guest visits, a subject for the later chapter on cleanliness.

Your decision as to management will go in one of two directions: impersonal (passive) management, or personal (active) management.

An impersonal approach is easier and will take less of your time. Guests will inquire or do an Instant Booking online. If they inquire with a question or requesting information, someone has to reply and answer their questions. Even if you choose the impersonal approach, you might be able and willing to cover this as it requires minimal effort on your part. The booking process, itself, is electronic and practically automatic.

Later in the process, requests or maintenance issues will be more demanding, require more time and effort, and may lead you to hire a management company to handle booking inquiries and what follows. Management companies greatly lessen your personal involvement, but they are unlikely to deliver the personal touch you can, and they likely won't be nearly as sensitive to maintenance cost management as you would be. They either have employees who address issues and they bill you separately in addition to their management fee. This could be a profit center for them with no incentive to minimize your costs.

The primary aim in managing your vacation rental is to more than satisfy your guests. Delivering an "acceptable" experience isn't enough. If you are to be successful, your guests must determine long before they leave that they are going to come back next year. Then they must go home, express exuberance in a 5-Star online Review, and share with their friends what a wonderful time they had at your property! Accomplishing this adds just a little more expense but noticeably more time and effort as to management. Eventually, your results will prove to be worth both.

This is where the personal approach comes in. Because I am retired and have the time, this is the option I took with our properties. I handle all the guest interactions, including response to maintenance issues should they arise, and overseeing housekeeping; my wife, Sandy, handles the bookkeeping.

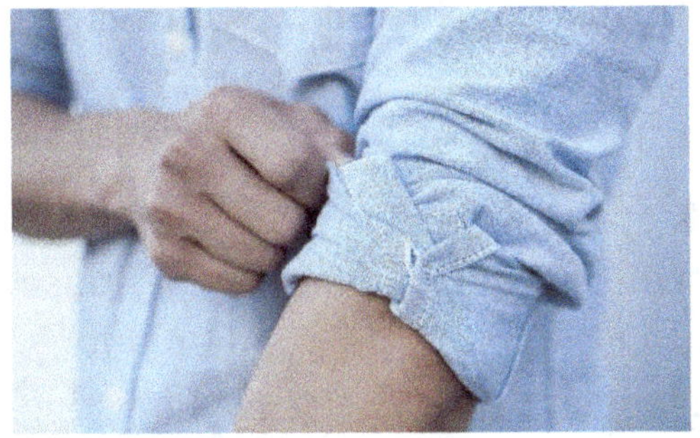

This approach takes more personal time and effort, but allows us to create, not just a higher level of satisfaction for our guests, but some "Wow" factors, which we will discuss in detail later. These result in more repeat visits, higher level Reviews, and more inquiries from future guests who are seeing those Reviews. This approach relates to the details of relationship management we will discuss herein.

The personal approach might include some or all of the following:

1) A personal "caring" approach to responding to inquiries and bookings, beginning with a welcoming phone call after the reservation is made.

Once the reservation is paid for, the listing site gives the owner the guest's phone number. A personal phone call from the owner gives opportunity to personally welcome the guests and to supply bits of information about the house or the area which can be helpful during their stay.

This personal touch makes guests feel welcome and considered and it surprises them; many report they have never had a phone call from an owner. Renting a vacation rental property can simply be transactional, registering in neither direction on

the emotional scale. On the other hand, from first contact, the experience can create a warm feeling for you as a host and elicit a noticeable sense of being considered for your guest. This isn't surprising; they feel considered because you are considering them!

2) A request for the guest's email address to allow a booking follow up email with your contact info, the delivery of House Access Info at the appropriate time, and other future communication, all of which won't require use of the listing site - the listing site is impersonal; this relationship now has a human feel to it.

3) A request for the first name of the spouse, significant other, or partner - this makes the experience even more personal and often helps with one or more of the "Wow" factors to be described later. When I ask for this, I just say, if it is OK with you, "Sandy *and I like to have both first names for our file.*"

4) A request for their drink preference - beer, wine, or soda - If you don't specify available options, you could get a request for Graham's 40 Year Old Tawny Port at $249.00 a bottle. That probably isn't going to fit in your budget and you'll be put into a position of having to turn down a request; head this off and prevent it happening.

5) A question as to if there are children in the group and, if so, what they like to drink.

6) A request that they use your cell number (for calls or texts) and your email for future communication - This is more

personal than notes on the online listing site. Your comment, *"Feel free to call, text, or email; we love to hear from our guests. If I am busy and can't talk, I'll tell you that and call you back!"* You will then provide your contact information in the welcoming email which follows.

7) Better Reviews - The phone call and personal communication is often mentioned by guests as a factor in their Reviews. They express feeling more welcome than in any of their previous vacation rental experiences.

We all know that we live in an age of ever-increasing technology, and we can learn to use that technology in ways that are beneficial to us and to our guests. While doing so, though, nothing compares to remembering that our guest is a living, breathing, feeling human being, and human beings like being considered.

A guest will almost certainly find your property using his or her computer, but that guest isn't a computer. Doing things which elicit feelings of gratitude and appreciation, things which stand out from ordinary or expected experience, is more than just beneficial. It can be the single factor that differentiates you from almost every other competitor in our industry. More on this later in the chapter "Include Wow Factors".

MAKE IT PERSONAL

We just discussed the personal management approach to handling inquiries and booking follow up. This isn't limited to the welcoming phone call; it can be extended through personal communication after the booking is confirmed. These personal touches go a long way towards making a guest feel exceptionally welcome and particularly cared for:

1) On the welcoming phone call you asked what they drink; beer, wine or soda. Have what they chose at the house awaiting them on their arrival. Have the red wine sitting out in a conspicuous spot; if selected, have white wine or beer already chilled in the fridge. Don't chintz! Make it two bottles of wine, a 12-pack of beer, or one or two 12-packs of the guest's favorite soda.

2) Have the children's soda or juice choice in the fridge or mini fridge for them. Take care of my kids or, better yet, my grandkids, and I'll love you forever!

In many situations, kids get overlooked. Having their favorite beverage there waiting for them is your chance to make them feel really special. Making kids feel considered will always register with their parents.

3) Keep a "Cancellation List" for guests who are looking for particular dates, but which are already booked in your calendar by another guest. Should these dates come available, you can contact the guest and let them know.

This management approach is more than adding exceptional things to their vacation experience. It revolves around a perpetual mindset of personal focus on the guest, and includes all the little things that come with it.

When Sandy and I visit one of the houses, we sleep in a different bedroom each time so we get the experience, personally, of that room. This has caused us to notice little things we never considered previously and we were able to correct minor issues or add little conveniences we hadn't thought about.

An example is small reading lamps on the headboards so guests can read at night without having to get up and turn the overhead light on or off. Another was discovering a loose toilet seat in one of the smaller master bedroom bathrooms. If we hadn't stayed in that bedroom, we likely would not have noticed that. You couldn't tell it was loose just looking at it.

This approach spills over into the financial picture as well, but delivers significant advantage to your guests with nominal expense. The overall effect on your bottom line is positive, though, due to exceptional Reviews and the resulting increase in your number of bookings! This approach places you at a "top of the mind" position when they book in your locale next year. This directly drives repeat business. For June and July'24, 100% of our bookings at our two properties on the Rainbow River in Dunnellon were repeat guests!

Personally taking care of guests does result in greater revenue, due to lower vacancy rates. But, the process itself, is also personally rewarding, in ways having nothing to do with money! Interacting with happy, grateful people who are enjoying the interaction is certainly preferable to responding to complaints and constantly putting out fires! Sure, it takes time and effort, but it is such pleasant and enjoyable effort, it doesn't seem much like work!

Sandy and I love reading the Guest Book comments, especially those written by children. One little boy wrote that his canoe tipped over. His final words provided great relief for us when he reported, *"But I didn't die!"*

Creating wonderful relationships is fun. Though brief, the interaction is enjoyable. Second, third, and fourth time around, it's like talking to old friends. Once in a while, you'll get a knucklehead who hasn't learned the lessons life gives us the opportunity to learn, but they are rare. The volume of wonderful, considerate, grateful guests greatly outweigh these few and the few are soon forgotten.

DELIVER A SPARKLING CLEAN PROPERTY

If your grandmother was anything like my grandmother, you've heard her say, *"Cleanliness is next to godliness!"* Never forget this. You simply must make every effort to never let a guest show up to anything less than a sparkling clean house! Nothing will undo the disappointment, the let-down feeling a guest will experience should they arrive at their house and find it hasn't been thoroughly cleaned for them.

It is irrelevant that your guest might not be Suzie Homemaker. Her house back home may not be sparkling clean, but that's her dirt. Any they find in your property is someone else's dirt, and it's in their home! For the time guests are in a vacation rental house, it is their home, and this connection has an emotional hair-trigger! You want it to be their home; that's what brings them back! If it is dirty, they aren't going to make it their home, and they certainly aren't going to come back or write a complimentary Review.

For years, when our kids were growing up, we rented a house on the Rainbow River in Dunnellon, Florida, where our two current vacation rental properties are located. Of course we

knew the house belonged to its owner. From the first time we rented, though, for the few days we were there, emotionally, it was our home, and if we felt that way a little, our kids felt that way a lot!

Guests are not going to be inclined to come back to dirty accommodations, and it isn't easy to overcome that! If I could better emphasize this by saying it twenty times, I would do it! Guests are not just disappointed if they arrive at a dirty or poorly kept house, they are "put out", irritated that a host would allow this to happen "to them." They take it personally and their sense of not being considered soars. Dirty, uncleaned accommodations are one of the most common factors in low rating Reviews. Even minor failures in this regard shows up in Reviews.

Allowing a guest to arrive at a dirty house will cost you exponentially more than their dissatisfaction and the opportunity to rent to them again. Future potential renters, seeing their reviews, will quickly skip over your property and keep searching, and you'll never know how many bookings you missed. This is the greater cost of your error!

On the other end of the spectrum is not only a clean house, but one which "smells" clean. The lingering scent of pleasant smelling cleaning supplies enhances ambiance and accentuates the sense of cleanliness. This also triggers an emotional response, but one that is vastly different from one resulting from experiencing a poorly kept property. One of our guests commented in their Review, *"The house was so clean; it even smelled clean!"*

Both poorly kept properties and clean smelling properties trigger comments in Reviews, but, obviously, different kinds of comments and vastly different ratings! This is your opportunity to positively influence the kind of Reviews your property is going to get; make certain you take advantage of it.

FOCUS ON YOUR GUESTS

In this chapter we are going to be discussing focusing on your guests i.e., being profitable. Another way of saying this is, in this chapter we are going to be focusing on being profitable, i.e., focusing on your guests! What you want to believe, accept, learn, and what you can come to know through your own experience, is that these aren't two different things; they are the same thing. Focusing on your guests is what creates profitability, and it does so better than anything else you can do!

Anyone starting a business does so for the purpose of making a profit. After all, this is the purpose of business. However,

once the business is up and running, if money is the business owner's focus, it becomes obvious to customers, and is not well-received.

If love of money is the root of all evil, a focus on money is its first cousin. We have all been in an interaction where the vendor was so focused on his commission or earnings he didn't even know we existed! It isn't difficult to detect this, sometimes nothing more than an uncomfortable "sense". When this occurs, it creates an unpleasant emotional state for the customer.

This experience isn't just unpleasant for the customer, client, or guest, though; it isn't exactly wonderful for the vendor either. When money is the focus, though likely unintentionally, the business person must try to obscure this, even if this occurs subconsciously. This creates an internal tension, kind of an emotional "tilt". The result is that the communication is either cold and impersonal, or it goes in the opposite direction, to obsequiousness, a disingenuous approach over-compensating for lack of actual consideration for the customer. This is uncomfortable for both the seller and the buyer.

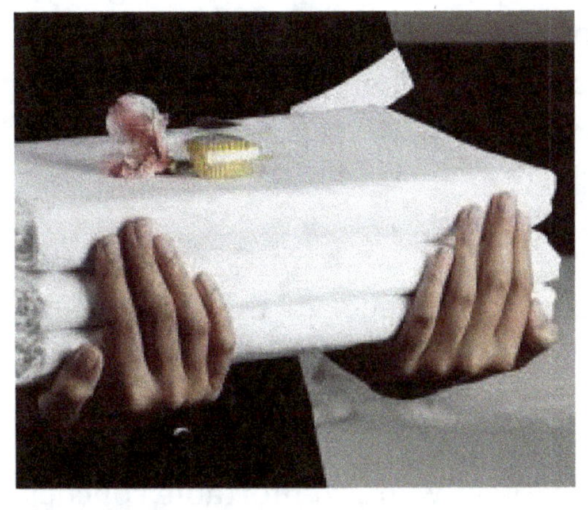

Guest focus starts before your first conversation with a guest. Consider the mindset of vacation renters - they begin to shift to a different mode of thinking as soon as vacation planning begins. They have already started to envision the trip, the destination, the attraction, the amenities, time with family and/or friends, perhaps a few drinks, relaxation, and a welcome slowdown in their busy pace. This is a substantially different mindset than the one they have the rest of the year. You want to make all you say and do align with this mindset and enhance it.

A personal management approach and one-on-one communication begins with making the guest feel welcome. Then, little tips and bits of information regarding the house, the locale, the attraction, etc. can subtly add to the elements of their excitement, making them aware of things they didn't know and things which will be included in their visit. As they look forward to these newfound elements, it increases pleasant emotional responses relating to the planned vacation, in general, but relating to your property and to you, specifically, and they haven't even arrived yet!

On your welcoming phone call you start things off on the right foot. Then, when the guest arrives at the rental property, everything experienced will either further enhance these pleasant feelings or will detract from them. **By the time the stay is complete, the guests will feel like pampered guests in a host's home, or they will feel like customers.** It isn't difficult to figure out which is more likely to result in a return visit or a top-notch Review!

* * *

There are basic things a guest expects in the design and furnishings of a vacation rental. These might include:

1) Comfortable beds

2) An entertainment area with a TV and comfortable couches and/or recliner chairs

3) Kitchen with cookware; cooking utensils; dishes, glasses, and cups; flatware; etc.

4) Amenities to suit the destination, such as kayaks or canoes, paddles, and life vests if a waterfront property

There are other things a host can provide that will enhance the guest's vacation experience, but which will be recognized as above and beyond, such as:

1) Exceptionally comfortable beds

2) Extra pillows on the beds

3) Even more pillows and blankets on the closet shelf of each bedroom

4) Coffee, spices, sugar, flour, boxed cereal, and other staples in the pantry or cupboards

5) A large TV screen and access to important sporting events such as football games

All of these things have a cost, but it is usually a one-time, infrequent, or nominal cost. Mostly, they require some extra time and effort, but they add to your guests' enjoyment. They make the property a home instead of a house. They make your guest's visit a memorable experience instead of just a stay. They make a guest feel welcome and appreciated instead of just hosted.

These inclusions create high level appreciation in the minds of guests as they recognize not only the inclusions, but the additional time and effort and the personal consideration that was required on the part of the host to provide them. You'll know you have accomplished this when you start getting Thank You cards from guests who paid you to stay in your property.

All these things are a good start but, if you really want to step up your focus on guests, go even further with the things listed in the next chapter, "Include Wow Factors"!

INCLUDE WOW FACTORS

We discussed supplying necessities and then some. We discussed going the extra mile, by adding the personal touch to your property management approach, and focusing on your guests rather than on profits. You are going to want to know how to go way beyond the extra mile, doing the exceptional, the unexpected, the astounding, providing an extraordinary experience, something your guests never saw coming and will never forget. You want to do things that will cause your guests to sit up, take notice, be remarkably impressed, and to rave about you and your property in online Reviews and to their friends. Last, but not least, you want your guests to visit your property again in the future.

First, though, let's look at an example which I experienced, personally, not in the vacation rental marketplace, but which perfectly exemplifies this protocol!

Several years ago, Sandy and I attended a business conference at the Fairmont Banff Springs in Banff, Canada. I am an early riser. Accordingly, the morning after we got to Banff Springs I was the first to show up for the first morning meeting. When I arrived at the meeting room, the staff was still setting up the room and the coffee hadn't been brought out yet.

I approached a gentleman who looked like he had some authority and asked if, even though I was early, it would be possible to get a cup of coffee and some cream and sugar. "Of course", he replied with a smile. A few minutes later a staff member showed up with a small tray, a small pot of coffee, a cup and a spoon, and small containers of cream and sugar. A bit more than just a cup of coffee but this is "service" in the hospitality industry and isn't unexpected.

The next morning, I was, again, the first to arrive at the meeting room, set-up was still in progress, and the same gentleman was overseeing the process, but the single-serving coffee tray was already there, with hot coffee waiting for me. This was "exceptional service", and was a little surprising!

The following morning, though, something extraordinary occurred, something I could never have imagined. When I arrived, the coffee serving was there again, but the man who had been in charge wasn't.

IT WAS HIS DAY OFF - BUT MY COFFEE WAS THERE WAITING FOR ME!

THIS WAS "EXTRAORDINARY PERSONAL CONSIDERATION" AND WAS NOT EXPECTED!

I was blown away! I have never been more impressed in my life, and I will never forget it! On the one hand, it was just a cup of coffee; on the other, it was being remembered and provided for in the midst of everything for which this convention center event manager was personally responsible, even though he wasn't even at work!

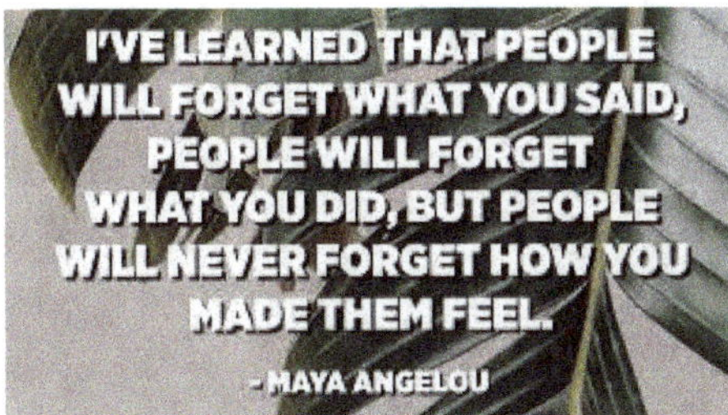

Did I write a letter to the establishment noting the incredible service and praising the Banff Springs Fairmont event manager for his exemplary level of personal consideration? You bet I did! The coffee waiting on me the second day, when he was there, was the extra mile. What occurred the third day was far beyond the extra mile!

As it happens, we have not had occasion to revisit Banff, but, if we ever do, there is no possibility we will stay anywhere but at the Fairmont Banff Springs! However, that isn't even the point. The event manager took care of me in an exceptional way while I were there. He didn't make one cent more for doing do; he just did it!

This kind of service reflects a level of, not just housing accommodations or hospitality service, but of emotional impact, and is included here because you can provide this level of personal consideration for your guests. You can make their visit like nothing they have ever experienced at any other vacation rental. One, or two, or three exceptional considerations, even little things, for your guest, their families, and their guests, will cause them to feel something, and will lock you and your property in their minds and hearts and, if they return to your area, your property is where they will stay. Here are some things you can do...

1) Without being asked to do so, make Early Check-In available when possible. When emailing House Access Information, include an attachment reflecting Early Check-In protocols. Explain that an Early Check-In is not possible when the schedule and cleaning protocols don't permit, but is absolutely no problem when they do. Explain that the house must, by necessity, be cleaned and sanitized for COVID protocols; these must be completed prior to guest(s) entry into the premises. Once this is completed, however, guests are welcome to come in, regardless of whether it is Check-In Time

or not! This is something which costs nothing to provide but is greatly appreciated.

2) Before your guests' arrival, if red wine was their drink of choice, place it on the bar or a counter where it will be seen as soon as they arrive. If they elected beer, white wine, or soda, put it in the fridge so it's already chilled for them. Put the kids' drinks in the fridge also, or, even better, in a mini fridge set up at their height. Again, it makes them feel how special they are, having their own drinks, in their own fridge! A little lax as to the sugar, perhaps, but their parents said it was OK and, what the heck, this is vacation!

3) After the guests arrive and have time to settle in, call and welcome them; ask if everything is good at the house for them; see if they have any questions; then direct them to a classy photo on metal reflecting the locale of the property or something associated with the nearby attraction. Tell them a quick story about the photo or the subject of the photo; then, tell them you want them to take the photo and the small stand on which it sits home with them when they leave. This always catches them by surprise, and gets a delighted response! (If you mention my name, you can get ideas for your photo and a reasonable price from Canvas and Metal Prints: 772 257-5918 don@canvasandmetalprints.com.)

Depending on which house our Rainbow River guests are visiting, we give them one of the two photos pictured.

4) They will be pleased if they find that the house has been decorated for a holiday. Christmas, Easter, or even Halloween decorations increase the festive sense guests experience during their stay; they notice it; and they comment on it! Nothing extravagant is necessary; just something that reflects the season. It takes a few minutes to do, but guests appreciate it and frequently comment on it in their Reviews.

5) Guests, and particularly children, are delighted when they arrive and find a small bowl of mini chocolates sitting out for their enjoyment. A little thing, not expensive, but one more way to make their visit to your property exceptional! Again,

these things have a cost, but not much cost, and they add to the "Wow" experience you are providing that they never got at any other vacation rental. This differentiates your property and you!

6) If your rental demand is seasonal, periodically, during low vacancy months, send your Email Listees a "Special Offer" with a headline: "For Our Email Listees Only". This includes all your past guests and inquirers, but doesn't include new potential renters who see your online listing. See details in the

"Create and Maintain A Rental Log" chapter. An offer of "Book Three (3) Days and Get One (1) Day, Our Compliments" costs you nothing but delivers significant value. Actually, rather than a cost, it gets you a listing you wouldn't have had otherwise.

7) Stock things at your property which relate to your particular location. We are on the Rainbow River, so we supply small, but effective, air compressors for guests to inflate their tubes and other inflatables for floating down the river. We provide water shoes, beach towels, and children's fishing equipment. "Wow" caliber components help your guests feel good, deliver exceptional monetary value, are likely to bring guests back, and contribute to exceptional Reviews which get you additional guests!

When these things are provided, guests aren't thinking about money; they are enjoying the experience and giving you all the credit. This is something advertising could never begin to deliver and, in fact, money can't buy in any arena. Sure, money can buy chocolates, but you are creating layers of emotional experience which guests connect with you, and money can't buy this. This, and the other things noted, are things that wouldn't be upsetting if they weren't there, but that create a "Wow" experience and an impactful emotional impression when they are! They make your guests feel good and they connect that feeling with you!

These guests will write rave 5-Star Reviews, express their wish that they could raise it to a 10 Star, tell all their friends about the experience, and come back and stay again in the future. All of this is peripheral, resulting from what you have provided your guests, the things that made them feel and say, "*Wow*!" This happens because you considered them! It is only natural that they consider you. You have created a personal connection and you and your property will be remembered. It is so strong that, surprisingly, guests will call you later and begin talking without telling you who they are; they will text you with no indication as to who is doing the texting. This occurs because they feel connected! Though they know it isn't the case, they feel like they would feel if they were your only guest. It's like they are friends of yours and, of course, you will know who they are when they call or text. They have you in their loop, and that is exactly where you want to be. This occurs because you recognized that they are special, and that is as it should be  because they are special. Isn't it a shame that bringing it to light is the exception! Isn't it wonderful that doing so feels good and just happens to be profitable!

Making a connection is a good thing, and you did it by recognizing that your guests deserve good things and then providing them! You have built a relationship in a genuine, caring manner and, by the way, that relationship will exist as long as they are taking vacations and you are providing vacation rental accommodations. Nothing could more effectively carry out your business goal of making a profit. Yet, you did it by giving none of your attention to making money, and all of your attention to your guests, and to making their visit exceptional!

The connection they feel is something which can't be bought. It has come from you, personally. You do these exceptional things as additional ways to consider your guests, yet, periodically, there can be an additional benefit to you that you never expected. Rather than explain it, let's look at an example that recently occurred at one of our properties…

Our maintenance lady, Ellen, is top notch, a real professional. She understands the hospitality industry and we couldn't have a better person filling that role for us. Once or twice she has caught a scheduling or calendar issue I inadvertently caused; fortunately, she caught it before it caused an issue for a guest. Still, we are all human and, though it rarely occurs, once in a great while something will get by her as well.

We recently had a guest who noticed that the areas behind the commodes were being overlooked, and the showers were, we'll say, less than sparkling. Following his stay, he sent me a note with accolades on the house, our communication, and his stay, overall, and, as requested by us, he included a note about those two minor cleaning issues. In the listing site Review, he gave us a "3" out of a possible "5" in the "Cleaning" category. However, he gave us 5 Stars on the Overall Review, the one that shows up and determines our Review Average in the Online Rating Metrics.

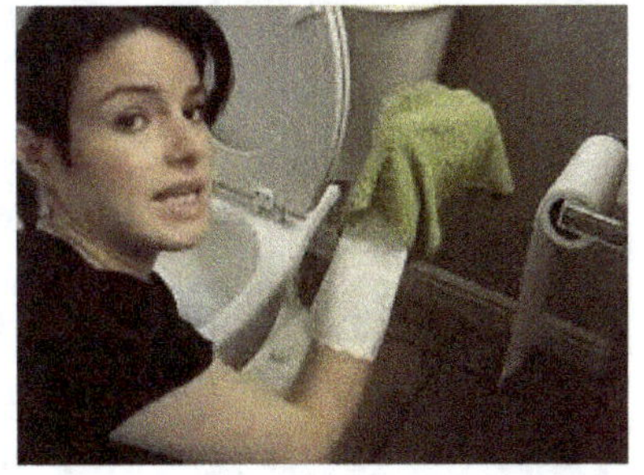

I was more than grateful for his consideration; it was absolutely above and beyond on his part! As to cleaning, that "3" was not out of line, and, if averaged in, it should have made the Overall Rating a "4". On the other hand, I like to think it was appropriate for him to give us a "5" in the Overall Review, but only because we had done exceptional things for him and his family in other categories. The personal communication with him, the extras he and his family and guests enjoyed, the

Comp Day we gave him up front, and the special gift we gave his wife to take home and display in her home, were all part of that. We did it to make his stay exceptional, but it sure helped us as to the ratings future potential guests will see on

the online listing site where he booked the stay! He gets all the credit for his generous consideration for us; we get credit for giving him a reason to be considerate!

For the record, we mailed him a check refunding his cleaning fee. When I requested his *mailing address, I thanked him for his consideration as to the Review. Here is his actual reply when he sent me his address: "It's (the refund) appreciated but not expected; we enjoyed ourselves and the conversations with you. Of course we would give a good review; you deserve it...We look forward to coming back again soon. Thanks again truly. We will refer others to you. Happy new year!"*

So, we got a top-tier grade! Not because we did everything right, but because we delivered our guest an exceptional experience, even though we slipped up and were guilty of two oversights. Isn't it the case that extending personal consideration can get us a top grade in a lot of areas in life; not just in our vacation rental operation?

We taught our children that "*Doing what you do, gets you what it gets you!*", and nowhere could this be more applicable than in the management of your vacation rental property. That 5-Star Review, keeping our average up in spite of a couple of atypical missteps, has an ongoing effect on the marketability of our property. Who knows how many rentals we will get with a Review Rating of 5.0 vs. a competitor at 4.9.

8) How would you like to deliver the most extraordinary value a vacation rental guest has ever experienced, without one cent cost to you? When your calendar has open dates that allow, sometime after the reservation has been made, but prior to the guest's Arrival Date (giving them time to adjust their travel plans), call them and ask if their travel schedule would allow them to take advantage of a complimentary additional night's stay. This allows a guest to arrive a day earlier or earlier than their regular Check-In time on their scheduled Arrival Date; or to stay until Check-Out time the day following their originally scheduled Departure Date, or stay as long as they like on their originally scheduled Departure Date.

This gets you and your property amazing kudos! Guests ask, *"What's the catch?" "Are you serious?" "Do you mean it?"* This is the extreme in the never expected category; it certainly has never happened to them before! This shoots their positive feelings about the visit through the roof. Since this is done after the booking is completed, there is no chance this is a day they might have rented. Without costing you a cent to provide, it gives your guests a gift with value equal to the cost of a night's stay at your property.

With an act of personal consideration, you have created an exceptional experience and an amazing emotional connection between your guests and your vacation rental and you, **and they haven't even arrived at the property yet!** This leaves them predisposed to love everything about your property once they do get there. When they do arrive, this exceptionally positive predisposition could cause them to give little or no attention to something about which they, otherwise, would have complained.

Taking care of guests in an exceptional way makes guests' visits special and more enjoyable, gets top-tier Reviews, and, thus, makes us and our property stand out on the Airbnb and Vrbo listing sites. Accordingly, taking care of guests in an exceptional way makes our vacation rental operation more successful.

However, taking care of guests in an exceptional way does something else for us that can't be measured. I get to experience guests' surprise and appreciation as each exceptional experience is revealed. I get to listen to them saying, *"Aw, are you serious?"*; *"Really?"*; *"Hal, That's too much!"*; *"And there's no catch...?"*; *"Thank you, so much!"* I get to read Reviews of our property that are in the top percentile of vacation rental property Reviews. I get the personal satisfaction of knowing we are delivering an exceptional product in the hospitality marketplace. Operating a vacation rental that provides an exceptional experience is downright fun and enjoyable and sure beats running an operation fraught with problems, constantly triggering complaints, and suffering low occupancy rates due to unfavorable Reviews!

A vacation rental business spans part of the time that makes up one's life. Providing "Wow" experiences fills that time with satisfaction and enjoyment, the things that make living life a pleasure. This is the icing on the cake!

TURN EVERY ISSUE INTO A 5-STAR REVIEW

With any business, problems are going to occur, and like all problems, they have the potential to be significant. The water pump stopped working; the heating element in the oven burned out; the toilet won't flush because a sewer line is backed up; the roof sprung a leak; these things are going to happen! **These issues are opportunities for your worst Reviews, but, at the same time, are perfect opportunities for your best Reviews.** The difference lies in how you respond to the issue. It is critical that you accept responsibility and spring into immediate action! At that moment, nothing short of a life or death emergency is more important!

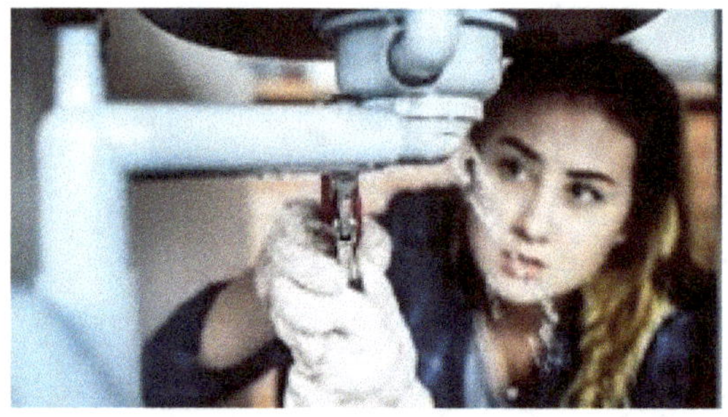

People understand that things happen; things happen to them at their house when they aren't on vacation. What matters to them at their vacation rental is that you care about them and the quality of their experience at your property. This is reflected totally in how quickly you respond and what you do to fix the problem! Next to cleanliness, an all-the-time factor, the next most crucial thing is whether or not you take responsibility and get an unexpected issue corrected now! You must understand that failure to respond at once with full and total corrective action can mean a ruined vacation for someone's family. You can't prevent the unexpected, but you can prevent it ruining your guest's vacation!

The good news is that, for you, whatever it is that goes wrong at your property while a guest is in residence doesn't have to be a catastrophe; as you will see, it can be a significant opportunity. Other than obvious ongoing lack of maintenance, guests don't complain in their Review because an uncontrollable issue occurred. Their response to the issue is, *"Hey, these things happen!"* If handled properly, the issue will likely either not show up in their Review, or will be only mentioned as part of their positive comments in their Review!

What will result in them blaming you is when you don't respond in the best possible way, in the shortest possible time, to rectify even a minor issue. When your response reflects anything less than total consideration for them and their issue, evidenced by your immediate action, they are going to blame you, and you and your property are going to get the bad Review with derogatory comments. I have seen these comments on other properties, *"When we notified the owner, he did nothing about it!"* or *"We contacted the owner, but it took forever for him to respond!"* When this happens, they will state the issue once, wax eloquent about the poor response or lack of response, and then deliver that 1-Star Review. It takes forever to raise your Review Rating Average after one of these!

If, on the other hand, you take responsibility (after all, it is yours to take), jump on the problem, and do everything necessary to remedy the issue on the spot, you'll be the hero in their Review. They'll either rave as to how responsive you were, how you saved them, and how quickly you did it, or they won't even mention the event! You will actually be more likely to get a 5-Star Review than if the issue had never occurred!

One of our two rentals is an "Old Florida" property, built in the 50s; that's actually part of its charm. While it's clean, well-furnished, modernized, and maintained, one characteristic of an "Old Florida" property is that it's old. We once had a faucet blow out in a bedroom bathtub in this house. Before the guest discovered it, water had sprayed onto the floor, flowed out the bathroom door, and caused the wood on the bedroom floor to buckle.

Once they discovered it, they called us. We directed them to the pump to turn off the water, but, by then, the damage was done. Three hours later, following a drive from Jacksonville, our maintenance man was on site, dried up the bathroom floor, and replaced the bedroom floor with new flooring. Their only inconvenience was being out of the bedroom for a few hours. Not only did we get a 5-Star Review, the issue was never mentioned in the Review!

During a conversation with one guest they made a comment that the master bedroom mattress was not comfortable and it

was depressed on each side of the bed. Before they went to bed that night a new mattress had been delivered and installed and the bed remade. Needless to say, there was no mattress complaint in their Review!

CREATE AND MAINTAIN A RENTAL LOG

The rentals you book online will be noted on those sites. However each will show only the bookings on their site. Also, neither gives you an Email List. It will be helpful if, beginning with your first guest, you enter their information into a Rental Log in a permanent record in your files. If you have more than one rental property, you will want to keep different properties on different pages. Still, you want your log to reflect all your rentals, including notes, and a separate page with a list of all your guest email addresses. I've found that an Excel Spreadsheet works great for this. Your columns should include:

1) Arrival Dates

2) Departure Dates

3) # of Rented Days

4) # of Comp Day(s), if any

5) Last Name; renter's & spouse's first names

6) Renter's phone number

7) Renter's email address

8) Renter's and spouse's drink preference (If they book again, when they do, reference your log and ask, *"Is ___________ still the drink of preference?"*, inserting the drink you provided last visit)

9) Children's drink preference

10) A note, or notes, if applicable.

Then, on a separate page, set up an Email List and copy and paste every guest's email address to it. This is for:

1) An occasional announcement in case of a high-demand in-season cancellation for dates someone would love to snag.

2) Every now and then, sending out a "Special Offer" to fill upcoming empty dates in your calendar. Rather than offering lower rates, I prefer adding a Comp Day to a stay. Revenue stays the same, and the house was just going to be sitting there empty anyway!

Retaining this information in your computer, backed up daily,

gives you instant access to all your guests. My experience is that storing your saved information on the Cloud is the easiest way to handle this. It is inexpensive and it's automatic!

MAKE IT EASY FOR GUESTS TO COME BACK

The best way to bring guests back for a return visit is to make their experience so exceptional they are not just satisfied, but are astounded with you and their experience at your property. Ways to accomplish this have already been discussed. After they leave, however, you have the opportunity to sweeten the pot even more.

One of the most effective ways to do this is to, following their visit, drop them an email thanking them for choosing your property and, in that email, offer them a "Direct Pay" option. This would allow them to book their next stay with you without paying online listing site service fees. Online listing sites get you connected with a guest who doesn't know you and is looking for a property. Repeat guests already know you, and they already know about your property. You don't need a listing site's services as to this guest; you already have each other's contact information. Provide an attachment to your email with "Property Information", descriptions of your property and links to the online listings so they can see property photos and current calendars (for available dates). Invite them to store this attachment in a permanent file and share it with guests who were with them and/or friends who might enjoy a stay.

Guests love this; obviously, it saves them money! This is just one more thing to cement your guests' wonderful impression of you and your property. However, while your guests will love you for offering this option, there are downsides, and they can be costly! The first is that it requires considerable time and effort to follow up on bookings, sending an invoice, tracking payments, reminding guests who haven't paid, making deposits, etc. This represents a time and effort cost, but the increase in repeat bookings might make this worth the cost. However, the second issue, a bottom-line financial cost, may not be worth the cost.

Online listing sites use algorithms that determine a property's placement position on their site. Obviously, it is to your advantage to be in the top twenty-five spots, or even in the top one hundred, rather than near the end of the last four hundred! Providing your guests a "Direct Pay" option can result in your listing position dropping to that extent!

Over time, your repeat guests are no longer booking on the site where they found you originally. Thus, permitting repeat guests to book directly with you will slowly, but definitively, diminish the number of bookings your listing site is getting for your property. Because of the algorithms, as your number of bookings decreases, your listing position on that site will drop further and further down the list. As your listing position drops, the number of new bookings decreases even further. Each is contributing to the other and while, technically, still listed, your property will wind up so far down the list, it is virtually delisted on that site.

It isn't actually delisted because it is there somewhere, way down the list, but for all practical purposes, it might as well not be. Your repeat visits will increase, but new listings on that site will drastically decrease. It can reach a point where, unless your property offers something so unique it will show up when the guest's filters attract it, like "Sleeps 15", or "Pet Friendly", it is no longer worth the price of subscription to that site.

I discovered this the hard way, experiencing a huge drop in bookings on one site and, while that was the case, my exiting guests were pleased, and the number of listings on the other site soared. This happened because of the availability caused by the fewer bookings on the first site.

One potential way of handling this is to notify the guests on your Email List that you no longer offer a Direct Pay option, but that if they book online, you will refund their listing fee. This will cost you 12% or more, but, if it is well received enough, the additional bookings may more than compensate for the cost. The other option is to simply never offer a Direct Pay option to start with, but that means missing an opportunity to strongly motivate your guests to visit your property again. If you elect the refund option, notify your Email Listees a couple of times to make sure they are aware you are doing it!

Another thing to consider is that, occasionally, a potential guest will find you on an online listing site, then locate you on some social media site, and contact you with a request to book directly with you. Should this occur, my suggestion is to decline the offer. Never go around an online listing service for a first booking for someone who found your property on that site. These sites are your lifeline! They have earned, and are entitled to their fee.

Periodically, send all your Email Listees an email just touching base. This keeps you and your property fresh in their minds. Advise them of events in your area, seasonal demand that might require an early booking, or anything else which brings attention to your area and your property. Following a guest visit, send your guest a "Your visit to (name of your property)" email, requesting feedback from them, asking them to let you know if there was anything that wasn't perfect during their visit. Explain that this allows you to know about things of which you weren't aware, so you can address them for your next guest or for them should they decide to visit again. Make certain that you convey that you want their honest feedback and that it helps you keep the property up to your exacting standards. This subtly reminds them of their stay with you, and can result in a new booking they "have been meaning to arrange!" Make certain that if a guest provides you with information on something that needs attention that, if it is something you are willing to change, you take corrective action at once. Another protocol which can increase return visits is to, in your follow-up email, provide an attachment to your email with "Property Information", descriptions of your property and links to the online listings. Include a suggestion that your guest save the attachment in their permanent files. This keeps it handy and keeps them out of search engines

when they are planning their next visit to your area. This attachment should include your property link for current calendars (for available dates). In addition to inviting them to store this info in a permanent file, invite them to share it with guests who were with them and/or friends who might be planning a visit to your area.

CHECK YOUR FOCUS

We discussed focus in the "Focus on Your Guests" chapter. Revisiting your focus relates to that, but is a separate activity. You might start with the best intentions, totally committed to delivering a "guest focused" vacation rental property. Then six  or eight months later, you have three maintenance issues in a row; an online site syncing issue which has allowed someone to book dates which were already booked; not a single reservation for next month; and the guest who just left trashed your property!

When this happens, it can be difficult to think about guests or remember to be considerate of them. I'm reminded of that old saying, *"When you're waist-deep in alligators, it's hard to remember that your original objective was to drain the swamp!"*

This is when you really have to check yourself and your focus. You don't want to allow a temporary bad event or stretch of events to cause you to lose your focus and not provide an exceptional experience for your next guest. For that guest, it's vacation time, and they had nothing to do with the previous events at your property. They are excited and looking forward to visiting!

These guests are about to deliver what you need most for your property - guests! Nothing that already happened can be allowed to prevent you providing this guest a phenomenal experience! Given what it can cause, the importance of this can't be overemphasized! It can, literally, cause a series of future vacancies you could have prevented! This is because one guest's bad experience can result in a bad Review and prevent visits by a long list of potential future guests!

If you manage your property the right way, it isn't likely that you will experience multiple troubling events. You will likely get a bad apple once in a while but, following the suggestions in this guide will make most of your experiences wonderful. The purpose of this chapter is to remind you to continue to do the right things, regardless of any past experience. If you have a bad issue, remember your chosen focus and renew it. Redouble your efforts to be the best choice in your area for guests coming to your area. If necessary, take a few minutes and do whatever you do to get centered when you find yourself off track.

Remind yourself of everything we've been discussing, and kick it up a notch. Think about the last guests who gave your property and you a 5-Star Review and booked their next stay when they got home! Then take a look at your mindset as to the current operation and management of your property, and recommit to what guarantees a wonderful stay at a vacation rental property, i.e., providing your guests exceptional experiences!

With this in mind, remind yourself of some of what we have discussed, the focus of this writing, and what must be your focus as you move forward. Continue to look for ways to deliver the most extraordinary vacation rental experience in the hospitality industry. OK, you might not be able to offer a house on a private Caribbean Island with glass floors and a view of the ocean floor under the house, but, you can deliver the best option in your market! By following the suggestions in this guide, you can do this, even with an unexceptional property.

Begin with the welcome phone call. Then check your calendar and see if you have the opportunity to add a Comp Day during a period when occupancy is low and you have available days to spare. Take the time to read the comments in your guest book. If you don't have a guest book, get one. A guest's contribution to a guest book actually increases their emotional connection with you and your property.

Surprise your next guest with more than they ever expected, more than they ever experienced before on a stay at a vacation rental property. You will not only have far fewer vacancies, the Reviews your guests create will attract the kind of guests owners dream about! Remember that a few dollars less profit per visit plus more visits translates to more total profit. Don't hesitate to spend a few bucks making your guests' visits exceptional. Empty properties don't make money; they cost money! Also, remind yourself that this formula is results-based and takes a little time to work.

Someone once said that the way you spell worship is "A T T E N T I O N"! So, when you do your mental checkup, what you want to ask is, "What's getting my attention; what is my focus?" "What are the tapes I play in my head when contemplating my operation?" It is easy to start counting dollars, but what will increase those dollars is maintaining a mindset of thinking about creative ways to make every guest's stay spectacular!

The blackboard note here notwithstanding, customer satisfaction is not your goal. Instead of guests who are satisfied, you want guests who are astonished by their experience at your vacation rental. If the options are "pleasantly pleased" or "astounded", the latter will deliver and insure your greater success!

You have a lot riding on your investment in your vacation rental. Don't take a chance that your guest found their stay to be "ordinary" while you were worrying about costs or profits.

Don't risk interactions which rang hollow and communication which lacked sincerity. Take a moment and remember that experience you had with a sales associate focusing on commission while interacting with you and make certain you aren't that person! Then think about a time when you were greatly impressed by an exceptional level of service. If you never had one of those, make sure your guests aren't in the same position after visiting your place.

Guests are never surprised by expected experiences; they must be there. Of course, you want to make certain you deliver the expected things. Then, what you want to do is devote your attention to making your guests' experience phenomenal! This is the message in this guide. If you really want to get good at this, have fun doing it. A few earlier references to the effectiveness of profit creating protocols notwithstanding, don't allow money to drive your operation. Keep financial success a peripheral benefit. Operations can be where your head is, but your guests must be where your heart is. Actually do it; don't pretend to do it!

You are charged with proper stewardship of your assets. The absolute best way of doing this is to make taking care of your guests a game you play, where when you do it better, both you and your guests win. It is a mindset, a very profitable mindset, but the game is far more enjoyable when your guests are your focus as you play it. Allow your experience to teach you that if you genuinely consider your guests, profitability absolutely does take care of itself.

To prevent losing focus, set up a monthly or a quarterly reminder note in your calendar to do an "Attitude Check". Every time it pops up, step back and look at everything you are doing. Review your actions over the last ninety days. Are you interacting with your guests beginning with inquiry? How many Comp Days have you provided lately? Did you find out what the adults and the kids drink; was it there when they arrived? Is the bowl of miniature chocolates on the bar or the coffee table for every guest? Do you advise every guest of your Early Check-In protocol? Do your communications sound like you're talking to a friend? Have you noticed anything at your property that needs some attention but hasn't gotten it yet?

If your property isn't performing, take a few minutes and ask yourself, what is your mental focus. Check to see if you are grateful for your guests' visits to your property. Objectively review your thoughts about your property and about your guests after they leave. See whether the primary subject of those tapes you play mentally is profit or guests and their experience. Think about a phrase you have probably heard before, *"As within, so without!"* If you find that money seems to be dominating the arena, read this guide again and take another stab at it. Again, let your results be your teacher.

The bottom line is to take care of your guests better than you would expect to be cared for, but as you would like to be. To see the kind of Reviews this approach creates, see: www.vrbo.com/730878 & www.vrbo.com/1482265. Take a few minutes, check these out, and pay attention not only to the Star Ratings, but to what guests are saying about their visit. Notice how often the guests specifically mention the host and/or communication. If you are already operating a vacation rental property, do it now before you continue reading...

It isn't accidental that taking care of guests works better than not doing so. Chatting people up and saying and doing things to generate profits is one thing; recognizing people as people like yourself, doing everything you know to take care of them because they matter, and going out of your way to surprise and delight is a completely different thing. The difference between the two can be subtle in its expression, but it isn't in its reception. Guests get it; guests get you! Sure, some people will be fooled by manipulation, but many won't. Some may recognize insincerity, but be glad for the services anyway, but it won't work this way for the kind of guests you want to attract.

Before we wrap things up, let's look at this from another point of view, though, not from that of the guests, but from that of owner-operator hosts. As you interact with your guests, you will always know where you're coming from. You can't be insincere with and as to your guests and not recognize it, and this is what generates your sense of self. If you are sincerely genuine and caring, with personal integrity in your deliverance of services, you know that. If being genuinely caring and considerate of your guests results in successful operation of your vacation rental, that's a good thing. On the other hand, if you are phony and disingenuous, even if you did fool your guests, even if your operation is financially successful, you can never fool yourself.

Owning and operating a vacation rental property is exactly like every other activity in one's life in that it provides one an opportunity to check one's perspective. Every endeavor, every project, every activity, every spoken word, even every thought and feeling, is opportunity for taking note of what's behind it, what's going on internally. My experience is that what's going on inside is causative as to all that is going on outside. Thus, the phrase, *"As within, so without"*, from the full phrase, *"As above, so below, as within, so without, as the universe, so the soul…"* This is found in The Emerald Tablets (Merchant Books, August 29, 2022), authorship of which has been attributed to Hermes Trismegistus, a legendary ancient Egyptian sage.

Regardless of source, if we find that our perspective is a causative factor in our life, and we can change things for ourselves by changing where we are coming from, internally, what a beautiful thing to discover. If we find that genuinely improving where we are coming from in the management of our vacation rental property makes our operation more successful, perhaps we can extend that into other areas of our lives, making them better as well.

I discovered this in my career, running our financial, tax, and estate planning practice. Switching from a focus on commissions to a genuine total client focus, literally changed my practice and my life. Starting with the same focus with our vacation rental management was a natural, and it got the same results as did the switch in my career. The true test of this is when we do slip, when we don't deliver, regardless of our intent and our efforts, do we make it good with our guests. When that guest finds that the shower wasn't clean and behind the commodes has been overlooked for some time, do we, without hesitation, get a mailing address and refund the cleaning fee?

Don't just start with a total guest focus, periodically check to make sure it's still there. Remember, the success that focusing on guests brings can, itself, be a detractor, resulting in a focus on the financial success which results from doing so. This is why it is important to step back once in a while and make sure we aren't distracted from what is important, what brought us that success!

BONUS

This guide promised twelve things to enhance profitability. Nothing will prevent or guarantee your success like Reviews, but there wasn't a chapter on Reviews. This is because it would be meaningless to write, *"Get Exceptional Reviews."* Getting exceptional reviews isn't a separate activity you perform. Reviews are the measuring stick as to how well you are doing everything discussed in the twelve sections that were included. This entire guide was about Reviews; that's why the words Review and Reviews were always capitalized. Reviews are the divine results of divine management protocols. This isn't a stretch; weren't we told to love our neighbors? This guide is about loving your guests, and if you genuinely do so, your guests will love you right back with Reviews which lead to more guests, repeat visits, and profitable vacation rental property ownership!

What you've just read isn't theoretical; it is a picture resulting from practically implemented protocols based on a total guest focus, and the Reviews you just read substantiate their effectiveness in a real-life environment. In addition to checking the Reviews, go back to the listings and check the calendars and note the completely booked months. These properties are river related properties, so the occupancy naturally decreases in the colder months. Accordingly, make sure you take a look at the Summer dates!

I would wish you luck with your vacation rental property but, if you follow the precepts in this guide, you won't be dependent on luck. Also, enjoy getting to know, though for relatively brief periods, some of the vacation industry's most wonderful guests. They are truly a pleasure to meet and host!

I genuinely hope this guide will prove helpful and deliver value to you exponentially in excess of its minor cost. There are a lot of things listed in this guide, but the best ones we haven't discovered yet. Some of those are the ones you will think of, once you begin functioning with a total focus on guests, their experience, their enjoyment, and ways to increase and enhance them all. You will discover touches we never considered, and, for the sake of our guests, and, yes, our profitability, I hope you will drop us an email and share them with us. These things will reflect your individual brand of personal consideration and we would love to hear about them. Between us, we will improve our own rentals, and simultaneously those of our industry, together, increasing the number of people delighted with a vacation rental experience.

I recently found this quote by Ray Croc online.

While what it says is well-intentioned, suggesting that you put your customer first, ahead of yourself, that actually isn't possible.

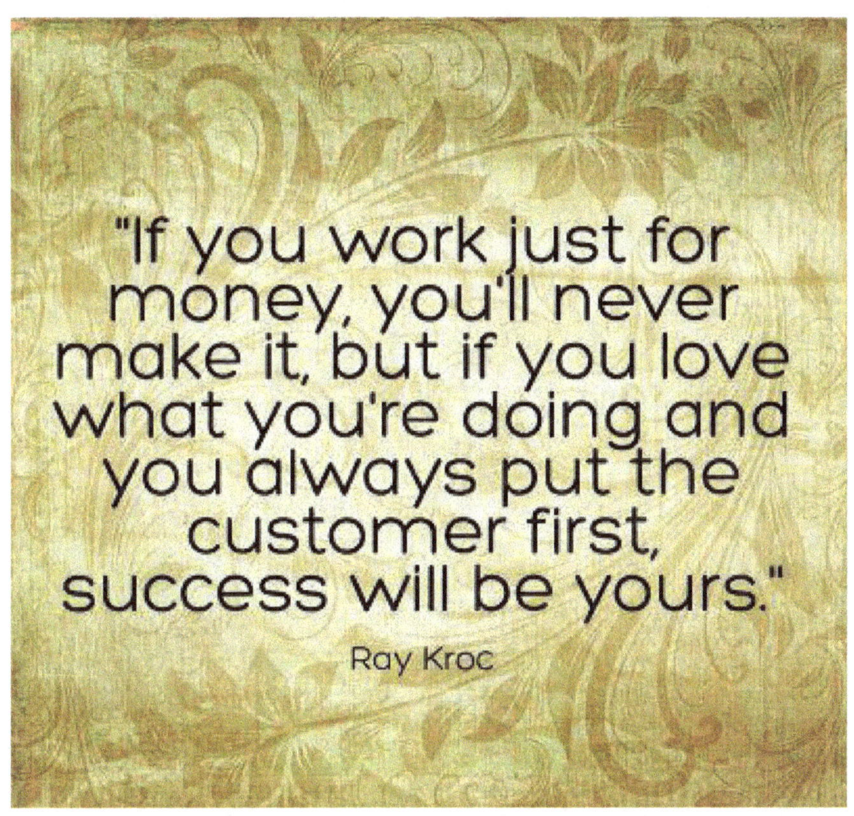

What took me more than twenty-five years to learn is that your customer's / client's / guest's best interest is your best interest! They are the same thing and, therefore, you can't put one ahead of the other. There isn't "your" interest and an "other" interest.

The absolute best thing you can do for you and yours is take care of your guests. Taking care of them is taking care of you! All that is left now is for you to do it! Make it your passion to deliver every one of your guests an extraordinary vacation stay experience; it absolutely is the best thing you can do for you and yours!

PROTOTYPE MANAGEMENT TOOLS & ASSISTANCE…

The mechanics of vacation rental operation is a different subject from that discussed in this guide. Operation details will depend on the particulars of your property, and what you will do, personally, vs. what you will have someone else do.

Prototype tools & documents that can be used in the operation of your property are available for a minimal per item fee – email me for a list.

Alternatively, ongoing input relating to your property operation and management is available for a small one-time consulting fee which also includes all of the available prototype tools / documents.

Contact Hal Rogers: hal@rainbowriverfun.com

ABOUT THE AUTHOR...

Hal and his wife, Sandy, are retired from their successful financial, tax, and estate planning practice in Jacksonville, Florida. Hal spent years selling financial products, during which time he spent most of his working hours overcoming objections.

After a major epiphany, he stopped all "selling" efforts and replaced them with a total client focus in his practice. He implemented a protocol under which he would not have a conversation with his staff, and they weren't allowed to have a conversation with each other, which they wouldn't have in front of a client. His practice became 100% transparent; what clients saw when they were with him and his staff was the same as what was there when they weren't present.

Using many of the concepts outlined in this guide, the practice prospered and life got easier and more satisfying.

At retirement, they sold the practice and bought a vacation property on the Rainbow River in Dunnellon, Florida which they named Chimera (Greek: "That which is longed for but impossible to achieve"). Subsequently, realizing what a special place it was and that people could be using it when they weren't there, they converted it to a vacation rental. Later, in order to offer a property to which guests could bring their pets, they bought a second property on the river, Meraki (Greek: "From the soul; that which is done with passion").

Hal and Sandy have been married for just over fifty (50) years, and have eight children and six (6) grandchildren.

www.ingramcontent.com/pod-product-compliance
Lightning Source LLC
Chambersburg PA
CBHW071503130726
47997CB00006B/2437